Practicing Catholic

Archbishop Daniel E. Pilarczyk

ST. ANTHONY MESSENGER PRESS

Cincinnati, Ohio

Cover photograph by Gene Plaisted, O.S.C.
Cover design by Karla Ann Sheppard
Book design by Mary Alfieri
Electronic pagination and format by Sandy L. Digman

ISBN 0-86716-361-5

Published by St. Anthony Messenger Press
Printed in the U.S.A.

Contents

Really Belonging

These reflections have their origins in a conversation I had some months ago with the pastor of one of our parishes here in the Archdiocese of Cincinnati. We were discussing the level of Catholic practice among his parishioners. He was disturbed by the relatively low percentage of his parishioners who come to Mass on Sunday. He spoke of a man in an invalid marriage who claimed that he had never been told that Catholics are supposed to be married by a priest. He said that he had met children on their first day of Catholic school who didn't know how to make the Sign of the Cross, and, even more stunning, that he had discovered school-age children of Catholic parents who were still unbaptized. We agreed that many Catholics don't seem to know what they are supposed to *do* as Catholic Christian believers. They are members of the Church, but they don't *really* seem to belong.

Of course, everyone who has been baptized a Catholic is a full member of the Church even if they never do anything as a result of their membership in the Church. They have the right to access to the sacraments, to Catholic teaching, to ministry from the Church, to Catholic burial.

Yet, while all those who have been made members of the Church are fully members, there are many members who don't seem to have much idea of what is expected of them, of how they are supposed to act as Catholics, of how they are supposed to express their Catholic faith and commitment in practice.

There are other members of the Church who are more regular in their participation in the life of the Church. They come to Mass on Sunday, at least occasionally, but they're not sure why. They want to do what the Church asks of them, but they're not always sure what that is. They want to belong, but their practice is sporadic and so they somehow see themselves on the fringes of the Church rather than connected to its center, and they sometimes wonder whether they *really* belong.

Then there are those that the secular media like to call "devout Catholics," men and women who are regular at Mass and the sacraments, who pray as a matter of habit, who are active in their parish and who expect to be "buried from the Church" when they die. They may not look on themselves as particularly devout or religious, but, if they were asked, they would acknowledge that they believe that they do *really* belong to the Church.

These reflections are concerned with *really* belonging, with living a Catholic Christian life to its fullest, with being active and faithful members of the community. It has to do with Catholic religious practice.

Of course, there is more to being *really* Catholic than engaging in certain religious practices. Being Catholic involves faith, receiving God's gift of himself to us, accepting what God has told us about himself and ourselves through Scripture and the Church, and responding accordingly. Being Catholic involves commitment to certain standards of moral conduct. Being Catholic means gradually acquiring a certain mindset, a particular way of looking on creation and human life and sin and suffering. These are all essential components of professing Catholicism.

Yet being Catholic also involves certain specific religious behaviors, certain religious practices which arise from Catholic faith and tradition and which, taken together, constitute a way of being religious in a truly Catholic fashion, a way of being members of the Church who are deliberately and consciously in touch with God in the context of the Church. This book is about those Catholic religious practices.

It has been said that Catholicism is as much a culture as a religion. In this sense "culture" means an integrated pattern of knowledge, belief and behavior that depends on experience and knowledge transmitted from one generation to another. It expresses the customary beliefs and social forms of a religious or social group. We all belong to one or more cultures: national, economic, ethnic; cultures determined by age and cultures determined by geography. The Catholic culture is that pattern of belief and behavior that gives us our identity as Catholic women and men, and "practicing" our Catholic faith means expressing who and what we are as members of the "Catholic culture," and, even more importantly, as members of the Catholic Church.

To be a *practicing* Catholic, then, means more than just being a member of the Church. Most fundamentally, it means giving external expression to our faith. Married people know that they have to express their love for one another. Otherwise it will be taken for granted and ultimately grow cold. In exactly the same way, faith grows cold without religious expression. But this external expression of our faith has to be ongoing and regular. It has to be a practice. We have to practice our faith because what we do not practice we tend to lose. Anybody who has ever taken music lessons knows that. Practicing Catholics, therefore, are members of the Church who consciously express their faith in ongoing and regular ways. They practice it.

It is significant to me that, when people say they have "been away" from the Church for a while, they generally don't mean that they have stopped believing, or that they have stopped being members. They mean that they have stopped practicing. "Coming back to the Church" means beginning to practice again.

There is always the danger of superficiality in religious practice. It is possible for people to go through religious motions without having faith at all. But I am inclined to think that going through the motions of Catholic practice is better than doing nothing at all about our faith. Religious practice can hold things together for us during periods when our interior dispositions are in turmoil. Religious practice is not only an expression of what we are, but a reminder to us of what we are supposed to be.

There is still another dimension to being a practicing Catholic. Catholic practice is indeed an expression and support of our interior faith, a constant exercise in being what God has called us to be. But Catholic practice is also a sign to others of our religious commitment. Obviously we do not practice our faith in order to impress other people. But our Catholic practice does say something to other people: something about us, something about the Church, something about the Lord. It gives some indication to ourselves to what degree *we* really belong to the Church (and to the Lord), and it lets others see what *really* belonging means.

I once knew a man who was not Catholic himself but was married to a Catholic. He raised his family Catholic and went to Mass every Sunday, but he never wanted to kneel during the Eucharistic Prayer because that was "reserved for Catholics." Sometimes catechumens who are participating in the process of Christian initiation (RCIA) will ask if it is all right for them to genuflect in church or come to make a visit to the Blessed Sacrament. It is not surprising for those who do not yet fully share the faith to wonder whether it is appropriate for them to share Catholic practices because they know instinctively that those who *do* practice the practices are giving witness to the faith that they themselves seek.

In the chapters that follow, I will deal with Catholic religious practice, with the fundamental religious activities that express our faith and our membership in the Church, that strengthen them and that proclaim them to others. There is, as I have said, more to being a Catholic than the religious practices that I will deal with, and there are more practices that Catholics observe than I will write about. But it is my hope that what I have to say will help people become more conscious of what their Catholic faith involves in practice and how the practice serves to strengthen and express that faith.

For Discussion and Reflection

- *How do you express your faith? Why?*

- *Has your Catholic practice changed over the years? How? Why?*

- *At what times and how has "going through the motions" of religious practice or observance helped you?*

CHAPTER ONE

Going to Mass on Sunday (and Holy Days)

I f it were a felony to be a practicing Catholic, what kind of evidence would be sufficient to convict somebody? Probably regular attendance at Sunday Mass. Regular attendance at Sunday Mass is the basic Catholic practice. Once you have stopped going to Mass on Sunday, although you are still a member of the Church, you really aren't a practicing Catholic any more.

The *Catechism of the Catholic Church* (#2181) says that "the Sunday Eucharist is the foundation and confirmation of all Christian practice." It is the foundation and confirmation of all Christian practice because of what happens at the Sunday Eucharist. When we go to Mass on Sunday, we gather with the Christian community in order to hear the word of God and take part again in the passion and resurrection of the Lord Jesus. Listening to the word of God and sharing the life, death and resurrection of Christ in the community of believers are the basic elements of our faith and so are also the basic constituents of Christian practice.

We need to hear the word of God because the word of God gives direction and sense to our human existence. God's word tells us who we are, what we have been given and what is expected of us. But participation in the Sunday Eucharist is more than a learning session. It is also a renewal of our sharing in the life, death and resurrection of Jesus, a sharing that constitutes the very essence of our being as Christian believers. Being a Christian believer means living the life of Christ, the Christ who spent his years on earth giving himself for other human beings, who died because of his faithfulness to his heavenly Father, who rose to a new kind of life that was extended to everyone who would believe in him and that would last forever. When we participate in the celebration of the Eucharist, we return to our roots as believers and are strengthened in the dimensions of our existence that give us energy and meaning. We need this renewal, and we need it regularly because it is so easy to let the life of Christ in us grow thin and meaningless. Without regular contact with the risen Christ we run the risk of forgetting who he is and who we are.

We also need contact with the community. We need to be reassured that we do not live the life of Christ alone but are part of a larger body in which Christ lives and teaches and sanctifies.

Moreover, our participation in the Sunday Eucharist is not just for us. It is also a testimony to others—believers and nonbelievers—of our faithfulness to Christ, of our communion in faith and love. When we go to Mass on Sunday, we are strengthened, and we strengthen others as well.

This is why the Church makes it quite plain that we are obliged to attend Sunday Mass. It's a sin to miss, not just because missing constitutes a violation of Church law, but because missing is damaging to my faith and harmful to the faith of others. My life isn't complete without regular contact with the risen Christ, and the Christian assembly isn't complete without my presence. "Obligation" isn't a popular word, but we are obliged to participate in Sunday Mass simply as a consequence of being Catholic Christian believers. It's part of what we have signed on for. Neglecting Sunday Mass is simply inconsistent with what we profess to be.

In this context it is appropriate to say something about the complaint of those who say they "don't get anything out of it." Sunday Mass is indeed supposed to give us something—God's word, renewal of our life in faith, contact with the risen Christ and with Christian community. But Sunday Mass is also a call to give, to give ourselves once more to the risen Christ in faith, to dedicate ourselves to the service of our neighbor, to offer our lives to the community of believers. If we only expect to get something, we are overlooking a major aspect of what the Sunday Eucharist is about.

This is why we are called to "participate" in the Eucharist, to put ourselves into what is happening and make our contribution to the action of the community. We are invited to sing, to respond to the prayers, to engage ourselves with the other participants, to engage ourselves with the Lord. The Sunday Eucharist is not something we attend, as if it were a performance that we may or may not find satisfying. It is something in which we have a part to play, it is something that we do, and if we find that we "don't get anything out of it," the reason may be that we are insufficiently conscious of what we are supposed to put into it. And that which we are supposed to put into it is nothing less than ourselves reaching out to Christ with the rest of the community, receiving his word and his love in the company of the Church. Just being there isn't really enough.

An important dimension of the Sunday Eucharist is its variety. Of course, certain aspects of it are always the same. There are always readings from Scripture. There is always the formal Eucharistic Prayer. There is always Holy Communion. But the tonality of the Sunday Eucharist varies throughout the Church's year.

In Advent we concentrate on the coming of Christ, his final coming at the end of time and his first coming as a child in Bethlehem. During the Christmas season we recall the events of the early life of Jesus. Lent is a season of repentance and renewal in preparation for reliving the death and resurrection of Christ during Holy Week and Easter. The Easter season recalls how Christ manifested himself after his Resurrection and how the Church started up and grew. The most extensive part of the Church year is what is called "ordinary time," stretching from the end of the Christmas season to the beginning of Lent and from the end of the Easter season to the beginning of Advent. These weeks symbolize the ongoing life of God's people, extending the life of Christ and headed toward his coming at the end of time.

The purpose of these variations is not to keep the congregation from getting bored, but to put the people in touch with all the aspects of the life of Christ and to allow Christ's life to color their own existence with the meaning of his existence. The Church's year invites us to apply the life of Christ to our life and to offer our life to him as it changes and develops.

"Holy days of obligation" are special feasts in the Church's year on which Catholics are also expected to participate in the Eucharist just as they are on Sunday. These feasts celebrate important aspects of our faith that, for various reasons, do not fall into the regular Sunday pattern. In the United States these feasts are Christmas, the feast of Mary the Mother of God (January 1), the Ascension (forty days after Easter), the Assumption of Mary (August 15), All Saints Day (November 1) and the feast of the Immaculate Conception (December 8). (Some years ago, for practical reasons, the bishops of the United States determined that the Mass obligation would not apply to these feasts, except for Christmas and the Immaculate Conception, when they fall on Saturday or Monday.)

The word "eucharist" means thanksgiving and, in the final analysis, participating in the eucharistic celebration on Sundays and feast days is about thanksgiving. When we go to Mass, we listen to the word of God with thanksgiving. We gratefully participate in the death and resurrection of Christ and receive the Lord in Holy Communion. We offer the Lord our joys and our sorrows, our problems and our achievements in gratitude for his share in them, and we leave the assembly thankful to take the Lord with us out into our everyday world.

Being a practicing Catholic means being gratefully in touch with the Lord. Our life as believers is supposed to be an ongoing act of thanksgiving, and that sense of gratitude is expressed and sharpened and nourished and energized to a unique degree when we come together each Sunday for Mass. That's why being a practicing Catholic necessarily involves participation in the Sunday eucharistic celebration.

For Discussion and Reflection

- *Why do you go to Mass on Sunday?*

- *To what extent do you "participate" in the Sunday Eucharist?*

CHAPTER TWO

Receiving the Sacraments

Next to going to Mass on Sunday, the most characteristic Catholic practice is what we speak of as "receiving the sacraments." This phrase is part of our basic Catholic vocabulary, but it's not completely exact.

For one thing, when people speak of the practice of receiving the sacraments, they generally aren't referring to all the sacraments (including matrimony, Anointing of the Sick and Confirmation). They are referring to Holy Communion and confession. These are the "regular" sacraments that Catholics know they are supposed to receive with some frequency as a matter of habit and practice. The others are what we might call "special event" sacraments.

Second, speaking about "receiving" the sacraments doesn't do full justice to what happens at Holy Communion and confession. There is a sense in which we "receive" in these sacraments. We receive the body and blood of Christ in Holy Communion, and we receive absolution in confession. Moreover, these sacraments (like all the rest of the sacraments) are gifts from God that we cannot earn or deserve. We can only receive. But there is also a dimension of "doing" in the sacraments. We are not merely passive recipients but collaborative agents in the sacramental action.

With that in mind, we can now say something about Holy Communion and confession, about what's involved in "receiving the sacraments."

Most Catholics treasure going to Communion. They gratefully remember their First Communion as an important step in growing up Catholic or becoming Catholic. They know that receiving Communion is supposed to be an ordinary part of attending Mass. They understand that, when they receive Communion, they receive Christ, "body and blood, soul and divinity," not just as a temporary visitor, but as a source of energy and direction for their lives. They know that Holy Communion is one of the most basic ways in which they stay in touch with the Lord and strengthen his life in them.

As a bare minimum, the Church expects Catholics to receive Communion at least once a year during the Easter season. If you don't receive the Lord at least then, you aren't really practicing your faith.

But receiving Communion is not something to be done thoughtlessly. The Church expects us to give some reflection and preparation to receiving the Lord. As an encouragement to preparation and to symbolize our hunger for the Lord, the Church requires that we not eat or drink (except for water and medicine) for an hour before Communion.

More importantly, if we have turned away from the Lord through serious sin, we are not in a fit state to receive him in the Eucharist. There's no point in trying to strengthen Christ's life in us if we have rejected that life through our own sinfulness. We first have to return to the Lord through the Sacrament of Reconciliation. This is why Catholics who have entered an invalid marriage and who continue to live together as husband and wife may not receive Communion. Objectively speaking, they are in a state of sinfulness, and that state has to be corrected before receiving Communion will do them any good.

But even more is required of us than the Eucharistic fast and being in the state of grace. As I said earlier, we have a part to play in the sacrament. Our part is to give ourselves consciously and generously to the Lord who gives himself to us. Holy Communion is a profession of faith on our part, a renewal of our commitment to Christ and his Church. Unless we are careful about doing our part in the Eucharist, receiving Communion can easily become a mere formality.

Sometimes Catholics wonder why those who are not Catholic are not supposed to receive Communion when they attend Mass. It's not a matter of denying people something or of being inhospitable, but a matter of consistency. Those who do not share the full Catholic faith should not engage in the profession of full Catholic faith that is implicit in receiving Communion. They cannot conscientiously say "Amen" to all that the reception of the Eucharist involves.

Now let's talk about confession. The Sacrament of Reconciliation is one of the more complex sacraments. Even the name by which we call it is manifold. The *Catechism of the Catholic Church* (#1423 and following) gives four names to this sacrament in addition to "confession": the sacrament of conversion, the sacrament of Penance, the sacrament of forgiveness and the Sacrament of Reconciliation. These names link the sacrament to Jesus' call to conversion and penance, to his offer of forgiveness and reconciliation with his heavenly Father.

In this sacrament the sinner comes to the priest to acknowledge his or her offenses. Presenting oneself for the sacrament is itself an act of faith and an act of confidence in the mercy of God. There would be no point in coming if we didn't believe that God welcomed us there. We tell the priest our sins and express our sorrow, and, in the name of God and the Church, the priest pronounces us absolved of our sins and assigns us a symbolic act of reparation for our sins.

Sometimes people wonder why they can't just tell God they are sorry for their sins and have God forgive them "directly." There are two reasons. The first is that we need to engage a representative of God in honestly facing our sins and to hear personally and immediately from that representative that God has forgiven us. The potential for self-deception is too great to settle for anything else. The second reason is that our sins have not just offended God. They have also weakened the holiness of the Church at large and thus offended all the Church's members. Therefore we not only have to seek forgiveness and reconciliation from God, but from the Church as well. When the priest gives us absolution for our sins, he speaks both in the name of God and in the name of God's people, which is the Church.

This communal dimension of the Sacrament of Reconciliation has become more clear through the communal penance services that parishes offer during Advent and Lent. We gather with other members of the Church. We hear God's offer of forgiveness proclaimed in the words of sacred Scripture. We confess our sins and receive absolution individually, but all around us are other people who are doing the same thing. Thus the Church teaches us that sin is not something just between us and God, but something that involves the whole community of believers.

How often should we "go to confession"? The Church's law tells us that, if we have serious sins, sins that have separated us from the life of Christ, we are expected to participate in the sacrament at least once a year. To remain deliberately in a state of detachment from the life of Christ and the Church for more than that signifies that we are not really serious about our participation in God's people. We aren't really practicing our faith.

But that's a minimum. Those who are in serious sin should seek forgiveness of God and the Church as soon as possible. Even those who are not conscious of serious sin need the sacrament because it serves to call us to attentiveness to our lack of generosity, to our selfishness, to our lack of concern for our responsibilities to others. Little sins can grow into big sins if we don't deal with them promptly. We probably should deal with our sins in the Sacrament of Reconciliation at least as often as we pay our bills or get our car serviced.

Often Catholics seem to give the impression that they don't look forward to going to confession in the same way they look forward to going to Communion. They look on Communion as a privilege and on confession as a duty, the duty of dealing with their guilt. But confession is not just about guilt. It is also about God's love and God's mercy, the same love and mercy that we celebrate in the Sacrament of the Eucharist.

The Sacrament of the Eucharist and the Sacrament of Reconciliation are about the basics of our Christian life: our need for God's love and presence and mercy, our sharing in the community of those who believe. That's why participating in them regularly is such a fundamental part of being a practicing Catholic.

For Discussion and Reflection

- *How do you express your self-gift to Christ in Holy Communion?*

- *Do you like to go to confession? Why? Why not?*

CHAPTER THREE

Praying

Praying is a less public and organized Catholic practice than the ones we have considered so far, but it is still central to being a practicing Catholic.

In its most basic form, prayer is consciously spending time with God. The classic definition calls it raising our minds and hearts to God. "Saying prayers," using set forms of words to address ourselves to God, is only the surface of prayer. What counts is what goes on in our hearts.

That's not to say that words are unimportant. They give structure to our prayer. They remind us of how to pray and what to pray for. They serve as a sort of primer for our prayer, to point us in the right direction and get us started. Sometimes in prayer we just don't know what to talk about with God. The prayers that we have learned by heart remind us of what we are invited to bring before the Lord.

The greatest formal prayer of all is the Lord's Prayer, the prayer that Jesus taught his disciples when they asked him to teach them about prayer. Saint Thomas Aquinas says that the Our Father teaches us what things we ought to pray for as well as the order in which we should pray for them. Every Christian believer knows the Our Father by heart. We pray it together every time we gather to celebrate the Eucharist.

Another important prayer for practicing Catholics is the rosary. In the rosary we pray the Our Father and the Hail Mary (the other basic Catholic prayer) over and over again as we reflect on the events of the life of Christ and his mother. As is the case with the Our Father itself (and with every other formula of prayer), the real kernel of the matter does not lie in saying the words, but in letting the words lift up our minds and hearts to make contact with the Lord and with the meaning of his life for us.

Then there are meal prayers, the blessing and thanksgiving we express when we sit down to eat. These prayers serve to remind us of our dependence on God and of the gratitude for his goodness to us that is one of the most basic factors in Catholic Christian spirituality.

Many of us were trained as children to say morning and night prayers, offering ourselves to God at the beginning of the day and presenting ourselves to God again at the end. Sometimes people "grow out" of morning and night prayers, and this is a pity, since all of us need regular daily contact with the Lord in order to preserve a dimension of meaning in our lives. For that matter, there is also the fact that all of us always remain children in the face of God. We never get so mature that we no longer need our Father.

One element in our night prayers ought to be the act of contrition, expressing our sorrow to God for the ways in which we have failed him throughout the day. The purpose of regular use of the formal act of contrition is not to keep us feeling guilty, but to keep us aware of who and what we are: poor sinners that God loves and stands ready to forgive.

The prayer formulas that we use are a kind of tool kit for practicing Catholics. There is a tool for every occasion, and it's good for us to have them handy. But the important thing is not just having the tools. The important thing is knowing how to use them to be in touch with the Lord.

Other prayers are more spontaneous: "God help me," as the truck bears down on us; "Thank you, Jesus," as the rain clears on picnic day. We can be in touch with the Lord for no particular reason, just because we love him, as we wait for a traffic light to change or for someone to answer our telephone call. Prayer means being attentive to the Lord whenever and however we can, attentive to the Lord who is always attentive to us.

Praying together is important, too. Jesus told his followers that, wherever two or three of them are gathered in his name, he is there in the midst of them (see Matthew 18:20). When a prayer group meets or a family says grace before meals, it's not just a matter of individuals relating to the Lord at the same time, but of a deeper and richer presence of the Lord in the context of their prayer together. We receive the Lord from one another and offer the Lord to one another when we pray in common.

Father Patrick Peyton spent most of his priestly ministry teaching people that "families who pray together stay together." This is because families that pray together weld themselves into a unity in the Lord that is even stronger than the natural bonds of family affection. One might say that healthy Christian families always require one more member, and that member is the Lord Jesus consciously sought and acknowledged in prayer.

An especially important form of family prayer for the Church is the Liturgy of the Hours, a traditional collection of psalms and readings that priests and religious are expected to pray as part of their vocation, but that is increasingly being used by laypersons as well. Some parishes regularly schedule morning and evening prayer from the Liturgy of the Hours. This way of praying has been designated as the official prayer of the Church in which the individuals who pray unite themselves with the Church universal in their attentiveness to the Lord. It is the family prayer of the Church.

Sometimes when people tell us of their crosses and their needs, we tell them that we will say a prayer for them. What does that mean? It doesn't mean that we will inform God of their situation so that God will pay attention to them. It means that we will stand with them before God in their time of trial, that we want to share their suffering, that we offer ourselves as God's instruments to care for them, that we acknowledge that their need is our need because we are all one in the Body of Christ.

It's the same when we ask other people to pray for us. When we do that, we are saying that we know that we can't make it on our own, that we are vulnerable, that we need the attentiveness of God and that that attentiveness generally comes to us from the Lord through one another.

Praying for other people and being prayed for by others are ways in which we acknowledge our interdependence in God's love for us. We are never alone. We are never alone even with God. We are always together in the Lord. That's one of the most important lessons of prayer.

Prayer is not some form of magic, the recitation of a set formula of words that yields specific guaranteed results. Prayer is not just an obligation that we are expected to fulfill. Prayer is keeping ourselves in touch with the Lord and inviting the Lord to be in touch with us, whether as a parish gathered officially in church on Sunday, whether as a family saying grace, whether as a group of priests praying vespers together before dinner, whether as a seemingly solitary individual quietly praying the Angelus at noon in an office or on the work site. Because the presence of the Lord is what gives meaning to our lives, prayer is the life's breath of the Christian believer.

To pray only occasionally is to make a weak and thin life for ourselves. To pray regularly, at specific times and in specific ways day by day, is to allow the Lord to play a major role in our human existence. To pray "always"—in every circumstance and at every opportunity—as Jesus commanded his disciples (see Luke 18:1) and as Saint Paul recommended to the early Christians (see Romans 12:12; Colossians 4:2; 1 Thessalonians 5:17) is to invite and allow the Lord to be part of everything we do. Being a practicing Catholic means being a practitioner of prayer.

For Discussion and Reflection

- *What are your favorite forms of prayer? Why?*

- *How is prayer part of your life?*

- *What does the Our Father teach us?*

Visiting the Blessed Sacrament

The Lord is present in our lives in many different ways. He is with us when we are at Mass on Sunday. He comes to us when we receive him in Holy Communion and when we celebrate his forgiveness in the Sacrament of Reconciliation. The Lord is with us when we pray. The Lord is also present for us in the consecrated Eucharistic Bread that we reserve in the tabernacle in our churches.

Originally there were no tabernacles because there were no Christian churches—buildings dedicated exclusively to the worship of God. When the Christian faith was given social and legal standing, churches as we know them began to be built. At some point, Holy Communion began to be reserved in the churches for the sick who might need it in preparation for their death. The reserved Sacrament was reverently kept in a special but not conspicuous place.

As the centuries passed, the Church developed new ways of responding to the goodness and presence of the Lord. Among these was the practice of offering adoration to the reserved Sacrament, to the Lord present—body and blood, soul and divinity—under the sacred species. As this practice grew, it seemed more fitting to keep the Blessed Sacrament in a more prominent place. Ornate chests and wall closets were used until, in the late sixteenth century, it became most common to keep the Blessed Sacrament permanently in a tabernacle, an ornate locked container in the middle of the main altar of the church.

About the same time, the liturgy of the Mass was growing more and more distant from those who attended. They no longer understood its language. Singing was reserved for the choir. The only thing that seemed to matter was that the Lord was somehow there. So, to the minds of many, the real presence of the Lord in the Eucharist became more important than the celebration of the death and resurrection of Jesus in the Mass.

People liked to look at the consecrated host. Priests were expected to prolong the elevation of the host after the consecration so that everybody had a chance to see it. In time, it became customary to put the Eucharistic Bread into a special container, called a monstrance, so that people could look at it and pray to it for hours or even days at a time. Seeing the host, at benediction or during the annual Forty Hours Devotion, became the high point of eucharistic devotion for generations of Christian believers.

The Second Vatican Council called for a refocusing of perspective. The center of Christian life was to be the celebration of the eucharistic sacrifice of the Mass, in which people heard the word of God proclaimed, in which they united themselves once more with the sacrifice of Christ, in which they received the Lord in Holy Communion. Attention to the presence of Christ in the reserved Sacrament was not discouraged, but was to be seen in relationship with the Mass in which Christ is with us as food, medicine and comfort, a presence to be assimilated more than contemplated. The adoration of the Blessed Sacrament was to be in harmony with the liturgy, to take its origin from the liturgy and to orient people to the liturgy.

Adoration of the Blessed Sacrament, contact with the real presence of Christ, even outside Mass, still has an important place in Catholic practice. It is an expression of the desire of individual Christians to spend time with the Lord Jesus, to cultivate a deeper personal intimacy with him, to make contact with the humanity of the Lord God in his nearness to us, just to be together with him as we are together with our friends. Almost spontaneously, when Catholics enter a church, even if they are there to see the art works, they will first find the tabernacle, genuflect and spend a moment or two in a quiet visit with the Lord. This is as it should be.

Catholics are glad that the Lord is near them. They like to think of him as having an address in their neighborhood, a place where he can always be found to listen to them and to spend time with them. Visiting the Blessed Sacrament, at least occasionally, is part of being a practicing Catholic. It is an acknowledgment of the accessibility of the Lord. He's not far off somewhere. His eucharistic presence is no more distant than the nearest church building.

Some parishes organize perpetual adoration of the

Blessed Sacrament. They arrange to have parishioners in the presence of their eucharistic Lord around the clock, twenty-four hours a day, seven days a week. There is never a moment in these communities in which some member is not praying for the needs of the parish and the diocese, for vocations, for social justice, for the conversion of sinners. This is a praiseworthy practice because it highlights not only our ongoing need for the Lord's intervention in our lives, but also the continuous desire of the Lord to be in touch with his people. Parishes that have perpetual adoration find a special vigor in their parish life.

Sometimes questions arise in connection with devotion to the real presence of Jesus in the Blessed Sacrament. Often parishioners will request their pastor to provide perpetual exposition of the Blessed Sacrament, having the Sacred Host always visible in the monstrance, and they wonder why this is not thought to be appropriate. The Church does not encourage perpetual exposition for several reasons. One is that exposition of the Blessed Sacrament is supposed to be a special event, a time of particular intensity when people gather in greater numbers to offer special adoration to the Lord. To make this an ordinary thing is to deprive it of its specialness. It would be like trying to have Christmas every day. Another reason why the Church does not encourage perpetual exposition of the Blessed Sacrament is that it tends to preempt the other activities that take place in the parish church. When the Blessed Sacrament is solemnly exposed in the monstrance, it is supposed to be the center of attention. Nothing else should take people's attention away from it. This is hard to reconcile with the ongoing activities of a parish church, such as Masses and weddings and funerals.

Another question that arises in connection with devotion to the real presence is the positioning of the tabernacle in our churches. Many of us grew up accustomed to having the tabernacle on the main altar, the center of the congregation's attention. This was not inappropriate when the priest celebrated the Eucharist with his back to the people, facing the tabernacle. But when it became customary for the celebrant to face the people so as to symbolize his contact with them as representative of Christ, he would often find himself with his back to the reserved Sacrament. Moreover, having the tabernacle on or behind the altar made for two different centers of attention when Mass was being celebrated. For these reasons it is now customary, when churches are built or renovated, to provide another place for the tabernacle, away from the main altar. The purpose is not to downplay the importance of the real presence in the church, but to make clear that the presence of Christ in our midst is manifold. One is the dynamic presence of Christ in the celebration of the Eucharist with his people, symbolized by the freestanding altar of sacrifice. Another is the ongoing presence of Christ in the reserved Sacrament, symbolized by placing the tabernacle apart from the altar where it can receive special attention. It is the same Christ, of course, but it is important to keep clear that the celebration of Mass and the reservation of the Eucharist are different aspects of the Lord's care for us.

In Evelyn Waugh's novel *Brideshead Revisited* (which many consider one of the great Catholic novels of our century), there is a scene in which Lord Brideshead tells his sister and brother that the bishop wants to close the chapel in their family castle. The teenaged sister, Cordelia, says, "We must have the Blessed Sacrament here. I like popping in at odd times." Our Lord offers himself to us as a neighbor whom we can stop in to see whenever we feel inclined, and popping in on the Lord is part of being a practicing Catholic.

For Discussion and Reflection

- *How would your life be different if there were no Blessed Sacrament reserved in your church?*

- *How does the Vatican II emphasis on the centrality of the Mass influence your devotion to the Blessed Sacrament?*

- *How often do you "pop in" on the Blessed Sacrament?*

CHAPTER FIVE

Doing Penance and Exercising Self-Control

The Church's formal laws of penance are relatively simple. From the age of fourteen, Catholics are required to abstain from meat on Ash Wednesday and the Fridays of Lent (including Good Friday). From age eighteen to fifty-nine, they are also to fast (that is, eat only one full meal) on Ash Wednesday and Good Friday. Substantial observance of these laws is a matter of serious obligation. Catholics are also encouraged to observe abstinence on Fridays throughout the year and to observe the whole season of Lent as a time of special penance.

The Church does not call us to acts of penance because we have to earn the mercy and forgiveness of God. God's pardon is not something that we can deserve through our own effort. It is a gift. The Church calls us to acts of penance because it is important for us to remember that we are sinners, that we have misused God's gifts for our own selfish purposes, that we are in constant need of God's mercy. When we do without meat on Friday or eat less on fast days, we are reminding ourselves that we owe God. We do without something that we could otherwise rightfully have in order to recall what we have wrongfully taken and used for ourselves. Acts of penance are not a payback that evens the score, but a way of recalling that we are constantly in God's debt.

It is traditional for practicing Catholics to "do something for Lent" beyond the little bit that is required of us by Church law. For many, doing without meat on the Fridays and fasting on Ash Wednesday and Good Friday are not really very significant, or are only a beginning.

The classical Catholic agenda for Lent is fasting, prayer and almsgiving. Fasting, in addition to the canonical fast, can consist in doing without some of our crutches for a while: the extra cup of coffee in the morning, the drink before dinner. Lenten prayer can consist in going to Mass each day, or praying the rosary on the way to work. Almsgiving (a rather archaic word for most of us) means doing works of mercy. This might involve special monetary contributions to the St. Vincent de Paul Society or an extra visit to someone we know in a nursing home. The important thing is not the specific practices that we undertake, but the heightened awareness of our need for forgiveness that the practices symbolize and the willingness to open ourselves up to the action of the Lord that they express.

Lent is an important season for Catholics. It's a kind of spring training or wake-up call that the Church gives us each year, an invitation to take stock of our lives and to allow God to put things back in order there. It's easy enough to overlook Lent, or to do the bare legal minimum, but if we settle for that, we are missing a significant opportunity to join with the rest of the Church in a renewal of our individual and corporate Christian identity.

There is another facet of the practice of our Catholic faith that calls for some consideration here, and that is the ordinary practice of Christian self-control or self-discipline. This is not so much a matter of actions that are meant to keep us conscious of our sinfulness, but rather of a way of living that keeps us growing and developing in the presence and action of God in our lives. If penance is aimed at dealing with the bad habits in our lives, Christian self-control is aimed at acquiring good ones.

We are all creatures of habit. Over a period of time, we do things in a certain place and in a certain way. We get up at a certain time in the morning. We change clothes when we come home from work. We grocery shop every week on the same day. Habits are ways that we have found to take care of the small change of our lives without having to start from scratch each time. Our habits become a second nature to us, but in order for them to take hold, we have to do them over and over again. Similarly, when we want to change habits, it takes extra effort and attention. Probably everybody has had the experience of turning down the usual street to go home for a week or two after we have moved somewhere else.

The practice of Christian life requires habits, too. We go to Mass on Sunday because that's our habit. We don't sit down and decide every Saturday what we are going to do tomorrow. We just do it because we have done it for a long time. It's now part of our life. We say morning and evening prayers and prayers before meals because we have always done so. These are our habitual prayers.

But at some point, the habit had to be formed. Consciously or unconsciously we decided over and over again (or our parents helped us decide) that these actions would be part of our regular existence. We took control of this aspect of our lives and disciplined ourselves to make it part of ourselves. If there had not been some decision and some practice, there would be no habit.

Forming habits is not necessarily easy. Other opportunities present themselves on a Sunday morning or we are tired when it's time for night prayers. The practice that seemed so right before now appears inconvenient or irksome. But we do it anyway, and the habit becomes a little stronger in us because we have exercised a little disciplined self-control.

Sometimes, however, habits seem to come about spontaneously. Without really realizing it, we suddenly find that we are late for work every day or that we don't have time to pray any more. This is because there is a kind of default setting within us that inclines us to that which is easy, effortless, immediately satisfying. We seem to be programmed to self-indulgence, and if we do not form other habits, the habits of self-indulgence will take over.

Basic Christian self-control or self-discipline is the way we keep control of our habits. We keep the good ones in force, we work at diminishing the bad ones, and we strive to acquire appropriate new ones. This requires a certain degree of attentiveness on our part. Committed Christians have always found the practice of a daily examination of conscience important for their lives. The purpose is not so much to keep ourselves conscious of guilt, but to take regular stock of our life to see where some attention is required. Did I pray today? If not, why not? Did I watch what I said when I was talking about the fellow worker I find difficult? What can I do to make things better between us?

The fact of the matter is that we are forming habits all the time, good ones or indifferent ones or bad ones. We need to exercise regular control over our habits because, if we don't, we may suddenly find ourselves with a whole load of unacceptable ones that we now have to struggle to uproot. It would have made more sense to deal with them when they were new.

The word "discipline" means learning, and when we say that Christian life requires discipline we are saying that we have to keep learning about ourselves. "Discipline" also means an orderly pattern of behavior, and exercising discipline in our lives means the constant effort to acquire a life pattern for ourselves that is in accord with who and what we are as Christian believers. It means deliberately putting our faith in control of our lives. We never reach the point where we can do without discipline or self-control simply because the Lord is always teaching us something more, because there are always new ways of responding to what God has called us to be.

Penance and self-control are not the same thing. One has to do with past sins, the other with present and future habits. But they have two things in common. One is that they are not always appealing. They can be demanding and difficult. The other is that they are both necessary to preserve a healthy realism in our life as practicing Catholics.

For Discussion and Reflection

- *What penitential practices have you undertaken during Lent? How were they connected with your life?*

- *What are your good habits and bad habits? How did you get them?*

- *How is Christian self-control a challenge?*

CHAPTER SIX

Getting Married in the Church

When we talk about "getting married in the Church" it's important to distinguish between the marriage and the wedding. The wedding can involve all sorts of things like rented tuxes and limos and the selection of the music, photographers and the hall for the reception. Sometimes people go overboard on things like this, but that's understandable since a wedding is an important event.

Marriage, on the other hand, is the reason we have a wedding. Marriage is the lifetime contract or covenant by which the bride and groom give themselves to each other in faith before God for the rest of their lives. "Getting married in the Church" means making this contract in the context of the community of faith. It's not essential, or even necessary to have a big (and expensive) wedding to get married in the Church. What is essential for a Catholic marriage is that the bride and groom express the appropriate commitment to each other in the presence of representatives of the Church (generally a priest and two witnesses). The reason this is essential is that every marriage is a Church event.

Marriage is a Church event for a number of reasons. For one thing, it's a sacrament. When baptized persons "get married in the Church," the action of Christ is involved. Christ enters the contract with the bride and groom and guarantees that he will be present for them to help them be instruments of holiness for each other and to see that they have the strength and help they need as parents of a new family.

Marriage is also a Church event because it is intended to exemplify the love of Christ for his Church. Catholic tradition invites us to look on the lifetime, faithful covenant of husband and wife as a symbol of the unchanging, ever faithful love of Christ for his community of faith.

Finally, marriage is a Church event because of the role that married couples play in the life of the Church. Our life in Christ that constitutes membership in the Church is lived out on a day-to-day basis in the family. Parents are responsible for training their children in the fundamentals of the faith, and this happens in the context of family. That's why the Church has taken to calling the family the "domestic Church." The family is a basic unit of Church life and is therefore important for the whole community of faith. That's why the foundational act of the family, officially entering the marriage relationship, must take place in the context of the Church.

Given the involvement of Christ and the responsibilities that go along with married life, it's easy to see why those who are conscientious about their faith, that is, practicing Catholics, are anxious to make their marriage a Church event.

The need for the Church to be involved in the marriage of its members is so important that, if a Catholic enters a marriage "outside the Church" (for example, in an exclusively civil ceremony), the marriage is not a sacrament. The couple may live together as husband and wife in the eyes of civil law, but they do so without an association with the Church and, for that reason, they are not welcome to participate in the sacramental life of the Church until their situation is regularized. It's not that the Church wants to make things difficult for its members, but that the refusal of the couple to put the most important human association of their lives into the context of faith simply disqualifies them for the ordinary life of the Church.

Given all this, it's easy to see why the Church requires a certain amount of preparation for marriage. It is customary in many dioceses for those preparing for marriage to be given some personality tests to determine if there may be problems that they need to deal with before they carry their relationship any further. Then there are marriage instructions, sessions in which the couple learn, or recall, the Church's teaching about the permanent nature of the Sacrament of Marriage, about the faithfulness and openness to children that is expected of those who enter the state of matrimony. Special questions arise if the couple is already living together before their wedding, questions about their intentions and about the probability of success in their marriage, and these questions have to be dealt with.

Here again, the Church is not trying to make things difficult, but is trying to be sure that the bride and groom really understand what they are getting into. If it's not inappropriate to expect people to get some testing and training before they drive a car or fly an airplane, it's not inappropriate to expect people to get some testing and training for their marriage. It's a matter of the Church's concern for the well-being of everybody: the spouses, their future families, the Church at large.

The Church is also concerned for the well-being of its members who have entered a marriage relationship outside the Church context. When persons in such relationships want to return to the practice of the sacraments, it is necessary first to examine the situation in which they find themselves. Sometimes these situations are easy to "fix up," for example, if the parties were both free to marry but, for whatever reasons, did not come to the Church to celebrate the Sacrament of Matrimony. Sometimes the situations are more complex, as when one or both parties have been in a previous marriage relationship. Then the Church must examine those previous situations to determine whether there really was a marriage, or whether there was some obstacle that made a true sacramental marriage impossible. For this purpose dioceses have matrimonial tribunals in which these matters are considered and adjudicated. Most of the time parties are seeking what is called "a declaration of nullity," that is, a finding that their apparent past marriage was not a real and sacramental one and that they are therefore now free to enter into a sacramental union. Tribunals are not Catholic divorce courts, but rather an expression of the Church's responsibility to uphold the seriousness of marriage.

The Sacrament of Matrimony, then, is not a simple and easy thing. It requires that those who would receive it be free of other marriage commitments and that they have the proper aptitudes, intentions and dispositions ahead of time. They have to go through the marriage instructions. Then comes what often seems the most difficult part of all: getting through the wedding and all of its surrounding challenges.

But that's only the beginning. There follows a lifetime together, a lifetime that generally brings a great deal of happiness to the husband and wife, but which also demands a kind of generosity and love that is unique to marriage. There are also the responsibilities that come with children, responsibilities of support and education and understanding. Having children involves a new level of self-sacrifice and, not rarely, anxiety. Once the children have grown, the marriage enters a new level as the spouses grow together into full maturity and old age. Marriage is complex and it requires continued presence and action on the part of the Lord as well as continued attention to the Lord on the part of the married persons if it is to be everything that it was meant to be.

Getting married is one thing. Being married is another. Getting married does not happen often in the lifetime of most people, and so it might not seem really appropriate to speak of it as a Catholic "practice," if a practice is something that we do over and over again. But being married is something that requires ongoing attentiveness, the habit of selflessness, and, often, of forgiveness, the practice of commitment and generosity. Practicing Catholics celebrate the inauguration of their marriage in the context of their faith and the faith of the Christian community, but they are also expected to live out their marriage, day by day and year by year, in that same context of the involvement of the Lord and the Church in their married life. Faithful Christian marriage takes lots of practice.

For Discussion and Reflection

- *What role have Christ and the Church played in the marriages that you are most familiar with?*

- *What do people have the right to look for from the Church when they get married?*

CHAPTER SEVEN

Raising the Children Catholic

Good parents take care of their children. They look after their nourishment and clothing. They provide the love and stability that is vital to the childrens' present and future well-being. They see that the children get the best education that the family's circumstances can provide. Because parents are the instruments of God's providence for their children, they want to see to it that they do everything they can for their offspring.

That's why parents who are practicing Catholics take pains to bring up their children in the faith. Catholic parents know that their religious faith is one of the most important things in their life, and they want to see that their children share that faith. It's one of the most precious things they have to hand on.

Their first responsibility in this context is to see that the children receive the Sacrament of Baptism. Baptism is the introduction of the life of Christ into our individual human existence. It is the door to Church membership. It is the foundation on which everything else rests. Just as parents are responsible for the beginnings of their children's natural life, so they are responsible for their introduction into the life of faith. The Church expects infants to be baptized within the first weeks after their birth (see Canon 867).

Sometimes problems arise with the baptism of children. The priest learns that the parents are not regular in their practice of faith, that their membership in the Church is not really important to them. Since baptism is the beginning of a relationship with God that calls for growth and development and nurturing, priests are unwilling to baptize children whose families do not seem to promise any support for the faith of the child. In these circumstances, the priest may deem it appropriate to delay the child's baptism for a while so he can help the parents renew their own religious commitment. This is not a matter of laying down a series of requirements for the parents to fulfill, but of helping them realize that baptism is more than a traditional religious observance that families with a past connection with the Church go through.

Baptism, then, is the essential beginning, but it is only the beginning. Once the child has been baptized, the parents must see to it that the child gradually becomes involved in a whole complex of Catholic Christian religious acculturation and education.

Most important of all is that the children learn that faith is important in their lives, and the most ordinary way they learn this is by seeing that faith is important in the lives of their parents. Parents accomplish this to a great extent simply by being good practicing Catholics themselves. They show their children what it means to be Catholic by their own religious attitudes, by talking about what their faith means to them, by letting the children see that the faith of their parents is important enough to merit self-discipline and sacrifice. Children do pay attention to their parents, even when it may seem that they do not, and often parents teach their children much more than they themselves are aware of. Faith will be important in the family in which faith is important to the parents.

In this context, just being together is important. Sometimes one gets the impression that contemporary family members spend all their time elsewhere than at home, with people other than their parents and brothers and sisters. Maybe families have to work harder at being together than they used to, but without some regular and extended contact, education in faith simply cannot take place.

But more than informal training in faith is called for. There have to be explicit attitudes and practices, too. In the home of practicing Catholics there will be prayers at meals and regular morning and evening prayers. The children will also know that praying is not just for kids, but something that their parents do, too. There will be crucifixes and religious pictures around the home expressing that the Lord and his saints are not far off somewhere but part of the ongoing life of the family. There may also be special ways in which the family observes Advent and Lent, Christmas and Easter, All Saints day and All Souls day, ways that highlight the presence and action of the Lord in the ongoing cycle of time.

Good parents will help their children learn that faith involves choices. What the children are allowed to see on TV or on the Internet, the words they use to refer to other people, the way their participation in organized sports is encouraged, the ideas of fairness, justice and care for the poor that they are presented with: all these are part of education in faith. They help the children learn that some behaviors and attitudes are acceptable to Catholic believers and that others are not. All good parents want to protect their children from wrong ideas about things like success, sexuality, violence, comfort and money. They do this most effectively not by preaching at their children, but by helping them form habits of making the right choices. Obviously the choices that the parents make for themselves also have an important educational dimension for their children.

Then there is the question of formal religious education. Our Catholic faith is not just a matter of appropriate attitudes and practices. It also involves a vast body of teaching, of explicit principles and doctrines that Catholics need to be instructed in if their faith is to be something more than sentiment. Likewise, children need to learn that their faith extends beyond their homes, that other families are Catholic, too, that other children are also learning what it means to be a member of the community of faith.

Our Catholic schools are an immense help to parents in raising their children Catholic. They provide not just regular secular instruction, but organized instruction in Catholic teaching. They also offer moral training and socialization in the faith. They offer a kind of linkage between family religion and the knowledge and practice of Catholicism in the larger world. At a time when many of the values of society are so contrary to Catholic Christian values, our Catholic schools have a particularly important role to play in the education of future generations of practicing Catholics.

Not all parents send their children to Catholic schools, of course. Many are unable to do so for any number of reasons. But the need for formal education in the teachings of the Church is still there. This is why parishes establish programs of religious education outside the context of school. Sometimes children are inclined to look on these programs as a nuisance, one more thing they are expected to do each week. Parents need to be wise enough to realize that these programs are a real service to their families because they provide so many things that families are generally unable to provide for themselves and give their children opportunities to grow in faith in a bigger context. In view of that, parents will do everything they can to see that their children take advantage of what is offered.

One of the most basic principles of Catholic educational philosophy is that the parents are the primary educators of their children. This is why Church leaders insist so regularly that parents ought to have some choice in the schools that are available for their children. But there is more to the principle than enabling parents to decide where their children are going to go to school. The primacy of the parents in education also means that the parents bear the primary responsibility in handing on Catholic faith and practice to their children. Nobody can adequately take their place. It is simply not right for parents to wash their hands of the religious training of their children once the children enter a Catholic school or begin to go to CCD classes.

Nobody can take full responsibility for the faith of

somebody else, and often there is no accounting for why grown-up children do or do not practice their faith. But practicing Catholics know that they must do their best to pass on the treasure that they themselves have received.

For Discussion and Reflection

- *Who had the greatest influence on the early development of your faith?*

- *How can parents best encourage their children to treasure their faith?*

- *How can you help the children in your parish to practice and cherish Catholicism?*

CHAPTER EIGHT

Being an Active Member of a Parish

All Catholics are members of a parish. You don't have to register. You don't have to make a financial pledge. Just by having a residence within a parish's territory, all those who have ever been members of the Church, all those whose practice is irregular as well as all those who are at Mass every Sunday are members of the parish, and all parish members have the right to orderly access to the sacraments, to preaching, to religious instruction, to pastoral care from the parish's ministers. Parish membership is not something for which people have to qualify. It's something that comes with their membership in the Church.

But just as there is a distinction between belonging to the Church and *really* belonging, so also there are those who are parish members and those who are *really* parish members. This chapter does not mean to suggest that those who are not active in their parish membership don't actually belong, but that ongoing, week-by-week participation in the parish's life, that is, being an active member, is one of the important elements of being a practicing Catholic.

The parish (like the family) is a basic unit of Church life for most people. They are married in a parish church, and their children are baptized in a parish church. They participate in the Eucharist there. Religious instruction comes to them through the parish. When they are sick, they are ministered to by representatives of the parish. When they die, they are buried from their parish. It is through the parish that most people relate to the full local Church, the diocese, and through the diocese to the Church universal. It's only logical, therefore, that an active Church life includes active involvement with the parish.

Most people belong to the parish in which they reside. In some dioceses, however, local diocesan legislation makes it possible for people to join a different parish if they choose to do so. There can be good reasons for this, such as convenience of transportation, or long-standing family connections, or special programs that are not available in the parish of residence. On the other hand, sometimes people will go to another parish just because they like the pastor there. But, whatever the reasons for going to another parish, membership in the parish of residence remains the norm, the regular way in which the Church wants its members to be in touch with each other.

There are reasons for this. There is a certain "givenness" about parish life that is expressed by belonging just because you are there. The Church universal is not a gathering of people who think exactly alike about everything, or prefer similar styles of preaching, or are all from a certain social class. The Church universal is the community of all those who have been called to faith by Christ. So also the parish is a more or less accidental mix of people brought together not by their preferences, but by their common life in the Lord Jesus. If "parish shopping" or self-selection becomes the norm, the Church runs the risk of disintegrating into preferential enclaves of the elite, in which other persons may not feel welcome because they are not like everybody else. That sort of thing may be appropriate for a social club, but it is not appropriate for a parish.

Being active in parish membership means looking to the parish for the fulfillment of our ordinary spiritual needs: the Eucharist, the other sacraments, contact with the wider Church. Because conscientious Catholics realize that these needs are ongoing, they are regular in their participation in their parish's life. They are anxious to benefit from what the parish has to offer, and they have the right to expect that they will find what they need there.

But participation in parish life doesn't mean just going there to get what we need. It also means giving, and giving involves much more than regular contributions to the Sunday collection. Of course, parishes need financial resources to carry out their work, but the call to give extends further than giving money to pay the bills.

What we are called to give in our parish community is ourselves: our time, our talent, our presence, our counsel, our creativity, our concern for others, our encouragement and support of the parish leadership. Being part of a community means sharing responsibility for the life of the community.

This responsibility that we share is not just for the sake of the community's well-being, either. Of course, the parish needs the gifts that its members are able to provide, but more than that, the parishioners have a need to offer themselves for the well-being of the community. We need to give for the sake of our own well-being because sharing what we have is one of the most basic ways in which we express our gratitude for what we have been given.

Being diligent in the gift of ourselves to our parish is a logical consequence of our faith. Christ calls us to faith, not because we are deserving, but because he is good. Christ makes us members of the Church community, not because we have earned it but because he is generous. And the only appropriate response to generosity is generosity.

In the last decade or so Catholic pastors have been encouraging stewardship. Stewardship is an approach to personal giving that suggests looking on what we have, not as our own possession, but as something entrusted to us by God. A steward is a trusted colleague of the master, to whom the master's resources have been committed, not for the well-being of the steward, but for the purposes of the master. A good steward is one who makes use of what he or she has been given to further the master's wishes.

We remind ourselves of our dependence on God, and we express our role as God's stewards by consciously and deliberately sharing our time, our talent and our financial resources with others as agents of God's love for them. This sharing need not be confined exclusively to our parish, but a significant portion of the sharing should be directed there because it is in the parish that we most often and most explicitly experience God's love and concern for us.

Sometimes people wonder what kind of financial assistance they owe to their parish. A good rule of thumb is tithing, giving one tenth of our gross income to charitable purposes, half to the parish and the other half to other charitable causes. People who tithe often find that their generosity to their parish and other charitable works results in still further blessings from God, broader and deeper than what they have already been given.

Financial sharing is the easy part. Giving of our own selves is more difficult, especially in times of stress and uncertainty in the parish's life. It is, of course, possible to walk away when things get difficult in the parish and wait for things to quiet down. But walking away is hard to reconcile with gratitude and dedication.

The parish is one of the basic Church contexts in which practicing Catholics express their faith. They are regular in their attendance at the Sunday parish Eucharist. They participate in the parish's educational and social programs. They pray for the sick and suffering of the parish. They are willing to lend a hand when they are asked, and even when they are not asked. Their faithfulness and generosity does not depend on their satisfaction with the way things are going at any given time. By their willingness to receive and to share in the parish, they encourage and deepen the faith of all of its members, as well as their own.

The reason the Church "assigns" each one of us to a parish community is because we need community in order to be Catholic. Our faith can't survive without it.

The Church also assigns each one of us to a parish because we need a context in which to contribute to the faith of others. They need our presence and our participation.

Practicing Catholics look on their parish as their home because they know that that's where they belong. And they know that home is not just a place to receive but also a place to give. That's why they are active parishioners.

For Discussion and Reflection

- *How are you active in your parish?*

- *What would happen in a parish if nobody but the priest needed to be active?*

- *What does your parish mean to you?*

CHAPTER NINE

Offering It Up

Some time ago a surgeon friend of mine was doing local surgery on a retired nun. She was not having an easy time. "Oh, it hurts. I need a drink of water. I don't think I can go on with this. I'm going to be sick." The surgeon was not happy with this and finally said in desperation, "Oh, Sister, just offer it up."

Whenever I tell this story to lifetime Catholics, they chuckle because "offering it up" strikes such a familiar chord in their Catholic memory. We remember being told by the sisters who taught us in school (as well as by our parents and grandparents) to "offer it up" when we had to miss the Christmas party or when we scraped our knee on the playground or when the school cafeteria served food that we didn't like. All the little trials of life seemed to elicit the same advice: "Offer it up."

Yet "offering it up" is not just an expedient for getting through childhood. "Offering it up" is an important part of practicing our faith throughout our life, and it involves not just trials and tribulations but gifts and blessings as well.

Many Catholics pray the Morning Offering as part of the beginning of each day: "O Jesus, through the Immaculate Heart of Mary, I offer You the prayers, works, joys, and sufferings of this day...." Even as adults, they are still "offering it up."

Deliberately presenting to God the events of our daily life is a way of keeping ourselves conscious that our life is not an accidental chain of meaningless happenings, nor something that is of significance to ourselves alone. "Offering it up" is a way of expressing our awareness of the presence and action of God in our lives. Giving our joys and sorrows to God involves a realization that they come from him, that he is somehow involved in them, that they are part of God's providence for our lives, that some dimension of everything that happens in our lives is a gift that we are called to acknowledge by sharing it with him in gratitude.

The joys of our life are easy to offer back to God because we seem to understand them more easily. When we get a raise in our salary or run into a friend that we haven't seen for a long time or find that something we have said has been helpful to somebody else or successfully bring a project to completion, it's easy to be grateful. It's easy to believe that God has been at work in these circumstances of our life. It's easy to present the gift back in gratitude to God's kindness and to acknowledge that it belongs to him as much as it belongs to us.

Of course, even this requires a certain level of attentiveness because we are all inclined to take good things for granted or to think we deserve them or to believe that they result from our efforts alone. We have to cultivate the habit of awareness of God's part in our lives, the habit of gratitude, and cultivating habits requires practice. Practicing Catholics strive to be habitually grateful for the obvious blessings they discover in their lives and to offer them back to the Lord.

Other things are less easy to offer up. The sudden death of a loved one, a serious illness, severe financial problems, mistreatment from a colleague, ongoing tension in a marriage: these are grave and painful matters, and it's often hard to see how they could possibly be part of God's care for us or how God could be pleased by receiving them from us as an offering. But Catholics offer these things up, too.

Spiritual writers speak of the "mystery" of suffering, in part because suffering doesn't admit of easy explanations. But it's important to realize that, in a Christian context, "mystery" is not merely something we find hard to understand, but also an ongoing revelation of God's loving providence for us.

In order to come to grips with the mystery of suffering in our lives, we have to look to the mystery of suffering in the life of Jesus. Here was a man who was totally virtuous, totally without sin, totally dedicated to doing the will of God, who yet suffered misunderstanding and scorn and rejection, who was abandoned by his friends, and who was put to death as a common criminal. Yet his was the life that brought redemption to all humankind, not because it was a life of suffering, but because the suffering was a result of his faithfulness to God and was accepted by him as a consequence of that faithfulness.

Jesus saved us by demonstrating to us what faithfulness can involve, by making up for the unfaithfulness of others (including ourselves) and by enabling us, through faith, to participate in and extend his life of self-giving and dedication to the Father through our own life.

What does the life of Jesus teach us about the mystery of suffering? For one thing, it teaches us that suffering is not always a punishment. Sometimes we do bring our sufferings on ourselves, but pain and sorrow also come to the innocent, as they came to Jesus, and when they come to us, it doesn't necessarily mean that God is trying to repay us for wrongdoing or that we are immediately responsible for everything that happens to us.

The life of Jesus also teaches us that suffering is not just suffering, a necessary but meaningless element in ordinary human existence. There can be significance to suffering, as there was significance to the suffering of Jesus. The suffering we experience as Christian believers, therefore, is not just a negative interlude in our individual existence, but somehow a sharing in the experience of Christ, whose life we share. Our task is not to understand it but to accept it in faith and then let God work out how it all fits together.

Finally, the life and suffering of Jesus also teach us that we do not suffer alone. Because Christ shares the life of all those who have faith in him, the pain of the individual believer is also somehow the pain of Christ. He unites our suffering to his. Then, too, the patience and faith-filled dedication with which the individual believer bears his or her suffering also contribute something to the lives of all the others who share the life of Christ. Somehow our faithful suffering strengthens the well-being of the whole community of faith.

All that having been said, suffering is still painful and perplexing. It is still a mystery. That's why we offer it up. We don't fully understand the reason for it nor its details. We don't rejoice in it. We don't welcome it. We merely present it to God in faith, hope and love with the confidence that the life of Christ is somehow at work here and that, just as his suffering brought grace and redemption to the world, so also our suffering will somehow contribute to our life and happiness and to the life and happiness of those who share his life with us.

The alternatives to offering up our sufferings with and to the suffering Christ are self-pity, bitterness, ongoing confusion and a lack of meaning and depth in our lives. We can try to rebel against it, we can grit our teeth and just get through it, or we can invite the Lord to make it for us an occasion of increase in faith and peace for ourselves and for others, something worth offering to him.

"Offering it up" is more than a Catholic catchphrase, a bit of cultural slang, a superficial throwaway line that implies not paying attention to things we cannot change. Offering up the works and joys and sufferings of our life means consciously contributing them to the ongoing life of Christ and to the life of all those who share the life of Christ. It is a deliberate way of assimilating and expressing the meaning that our faith offers us in all the facets of our lives.

"Offering it up" is not something that comes to us automatically, even after the years of conditioning that some of us had from the sisters and priests and brothers in Catholic schools. It requires thought and prayer and patience and practice. But it's an important element in being a practicing Catholic.

For Discussion and Reflection

- *What do you have to "offer up" in your life?*

- *Does offering something up make a difference in the way you look at it?*

CHAPTER TEN

Being in Touch With Mary and the Saints

People who are not Catholic sometimes wonder about Catholics' devotion to the Blessed Virgin Mary and the other saints. Catholic churches generally contain pictures and statues of Mary and the saints, often with vigil lights burning in front of them. Catholics will talk about their patron saints, or about praying to Saint Anthony when they have lost something. Sometimes they go on pilgrimage to Fatima or Lourdes or to the shrine of Saint Anne de Beaupre in Canada. Occasionally it seems that Catholics are more at home with the saints than they are with the Lord.

Being in touch with Mary and the saints is one of the distinguishing elements of the Catholic culture. It's an important part of being a practicing Catholic. There are several fundamental insights behind Catholic devotion to the saints.

First of all, we are dealing with a kind of family matter here. Being Catholic means being in a family, and being in a family means having relatives. Our relatives as members of the Church include not only our brother Jesus, but all his brothers and sisters as well. Most of these brothers and sisters are pretty much the same as we are, ordinary people without anything special to recommend them—except their membership in the family. Others are quite special, the really successful members of the family to whom we others look with particular affection and regard. These are the ones we call the saints. Practicing Catholics are generally attentive to their relatives.

Implicit in this family attentiveness is the conviction that the saints are not just figures from history that we look back on with admiration and gratitude. They are still alive with and in the risen Lord in heaven. Their life continues, although in a form that is different from their earthly existence. And because our life of faith is also a sharing in the life of the risen Christ, we are in contact with the Lord's saints in and through him.

But that's not all. Just as we are in touch with the saints through the life of Jesus that we share, so they are in touch with us. They love us in him and care for us in him. They don't look down on us from heaven as detached spectators of what's going on here in our lives, but as our brothers and sisters who are looking out for those they love. Just as the life and love of Jesus is expressed and extended on earth by those who live in faith, so also the life and love of Jesus is expressed and extended from heaven by those who live in glory. Just as the family of the Lord is not limited by place, but extends throughout the earth, so also the family of the Lord is not limited by time and by the presence of its members in earthly life.

Catholic devotion to Mary and the other saints and Catholic confidence in the intercession and help of the saints for us are ways in which we express our family awareness and loyalty. Being Catholic is never a matter of just me and Jesus. It's always we and Jesus, and the "we" includes Mary, the Mother of God, and all the other saints. We're all part of the same family. We somehow all belong together.

The most honored of the saints is Mary, the Mother of God. Mary is, in many ways the original saint because she came to know and accept Jesus first of all. She shared his life from beginning to end and now occupies a special place with him in heaven. Because of her special place in the earthly and risen life of Jesus, she has a special place in the Lord's family. Because she is Jesus' mother, she is everybody else's mother, too.

Catholics pray to Mary under many different titles: Mother of Mercy, Mother of Good Counsel, Refuge of Sinners, Queen of Peace. In fact there is a special prayer, the Litany of the Blessed Mother, that contains nearly fifty different titles under which Mary is invoked. This richness of address indicates the breadth and variety of Mary's virtues. It also expresses that Catholics look on Mary in many different lights, under many aspects, depending on our state at any given time and the needs for which we are asking her help. Mary's many titles also suggest that there is so much to admire and imitate about our mother that one way of speaking of her simply isn't enough.

Then there are the other saints, almost without number. One of the learned works on the saints runs to twelve large volumes, and a handbook that gives special attention to saints of the English-speaking world runs to 514 pages and contains about 1,500 entries. There are all kinds of saints: popes and bishops and priests, laywomen and men, religious sisters and brothers and monks. There are saints that were kings and emperors, and saints who were beggars, saints who astounded the world with their learning and saints who couldn't read and write. Perhaps one of the most fascinating factors of this great family to which we belong is its variety. You don't have to be of a certain personality type to be a saint. You don't have to come from a certain country. You don't have to have undertaken a certain prescribed set of religious practices. The one thing that all saints have in common, both those who have been officially declared saints by the Church through the process of canonization, and the other citizens of heaven who have not received official attention, is their love for the Lord Jesus and their dedication to him. Given that, the only limits to the variety of the saints are the limits of human diversity.

That's probably why every Catholic has his or her own favorite saints. Some saints seem more attractive to us because we find them somehow like ourselves. Perhaps they were interested in the same things we find interesting, or they had to deal with some of the same crosses that we carry. Most of us know something about the saints whose names we received in Baptism or Confirmation, and we like to think that they are especially interested in us.

Then there are the specialists, those who, for some reason or other, have been approached by Catholic believers over the centuries in times of special need or in particular circumstances: Saint Luke, the patron of physicians; Saint Francis de Sales, the patron of authors; Saint Lucy for diseases of the eyes; Saint Dymphna for mental disorders; Saint Francis of Assisi, patron of ecologists; and, of course, Saint Anthony for finding things that we have lost. They are all part of the family, like favorite aunts or cousins, and they are all interested in the other members of the family.

Catholics express their devotion to Mary and the saints in many different ways. They offer prayers to them. They visit their statues in churches, sometimes lighting a vigil light to represent their needs. They treat them with a certain degree of familiarity: "I'll have to talk to Saint Jude about that."

Many Catholics are able to visit the shrines of the saints, particular places where devotion is expressed in a special way. Often people look on shrines as places you go to get cured of illness. Lourdes, for example, is a sanctuary of the Blessed Mother that is much frequented by sick people. But when people visit shrines, even though they may have their own special agenda, they also realize that the Blessed Mother or the saint may respond to their prayers in ways other than what they expect. Not everyone who visits Lourdes comes home cured, but there are few who leave there without some sense of healing and a deepened understanding of the Lord's action in their lives.

Catholics do not offer the same kind of reverence to the saints that they offer to God. The saints can never take the place of Jesus, precisely because it is the life of Jesus that constitutes the common element that keeps the family together. Without him there would be no family. But there is a family, his family of faith and glory, and when Catholics pay their respects to Mary and the saints, they are offering their respect also to the One in whom the family has its origin.

Practicing Catholics are comfortable in the company of the saints. It's one of the ways they express their attachment to their family.

For Discussion and Reflection

- *Who are your favorite saints? Why?*

- *How do you express your attachment to Mary and the other saints?*

- *How does being in touch with the saints help you?*

CHAPTER ELEVEN

Being Willing to Be Different

In the middle of the second century, an anonymous author wrote a letter to a man named Diognetus in which he describes the situation of Christian believers in the pagan world:

> Christians are not distinguishable from others either by nationality, language, or custom. They don't inhabit separate cities of their own, or speak a strange dialect. With regard to dress, food, and manner of life in general, they follow the customs of whatever city they happen to be living in. And yet there is something extraordinary about their lives. They live in their own countries as though they were only passing through. Any country can be their homeland, but for them their homeland, wherever it may be, is a foreign country. We may say that the Christian is to the world what the soul is to the body. As the soul is present in every part of the body, while remaining distinct from it, so Christians are found in all cities of the world, but cannot be identified with the world. (See *Letter to Diognetus*, chapter 5 and following.)

Things haven't changed much since the second century. Being a believer today means that we may seem to be just like everybody else, but we are different. It's important for practicing Catholics to be conscious of where the difference lies and to be willing to embrace it.

Of course, there are some obvious and visible differences in the lives of practicing Catholics, aspects of their life that set them apart from other people and identify them as Catholics.

When you see somebody make the Sign of the Cross and say a meal prayer in a restaurant, for example, you know that that person is probably a Catholic. If the neighbors go to Mass on Sunday, send their children to the parish school and have a statue of the Blessed Mother in their living room, they are almost certainly Catholics because they do Catholic things. That's how you can tell.

But these identifiably "Catholic things" don't make them all that much different from the other people on the street. They wear the same kinds of clothes as everybody else, drive the same kind of car and take the same kind of vacations. There doesn't seem to be anything extraordinary about their life. Yet, if they are really practicing Catholics, there is something that is quite different about them. It's their values and their priorities.

Being a practicing Catholic means having a whole system of values that are different from the values of many, perhaps most of the people around them. This system of values helps them determine what is important in their life and what is secondary, what they are going to stand up for and what they are going to overlook. The way they deal with their jobs and their families, their use of time and money will be determined by these values and the relationship between the values. Practicing Catholics are people with definite and clear priorities, and often their priorities are different from those of other people.

The top priority for a believer is the life of Christ. As baptized persons, we have been given a share of the life of Jesus. Together with all the other believers in the world (as well as the saints in heaven) we are called and empowered to receive the life and love of Jesus in our hearts and extend that life and love to those around us: our family, our friends, our neighbors, our colleagues at work. That's what the life of a Christian believer is all about, and that's what is more important than anything else.

Consequently, maintaining and strengthening and responding to the life of Christ in us takes precedence over everything else. That's why practicing Catholics go to Mass on Sunday. That's why they receive the sacraments and pray. That's why they take pains with the religious education of their children. It's all part of living in Christ Jesus.

Our life in Christ, however, doesn't determine only our specifically religious behavior. It also offers us a whole set of principles and attitudes about the other aspects of our life. The way we think about success and failure, the way we look on other people, especially those in need, the significance we find in civic and political life, the way we view sickness and death: all of these matters are colored by the life of Jesus that is in us. In fact, every aspect of our human existence involves some connection with the life of the Lord.

These principles and attitudes that arise from our relationship with Jesus guide just about every decision that practicing Catholics are asked to make. What kind of employment will we accept, and how far are we willing to go to comply with what is asked of us in our work? To what extent do we respond to our consumer culture that keeps telling us to buy and use and throw away and buy some more? How important is it for the children to be on the soccer team? Do we watch the same TV programs as everybody else? Our lives are full of decisions, and those decisions are made on the basis of some sort of values, conscious or unconscious. For the practicing Catholic, there is no question about what the values must be: They must be the values of Christ, the values that Christ offers us through his Church.

These values are not necessarily the values of the world around us. We may not live in a militantly pagan world as Diognetus did, where being a Christian could cost you your life, but there is enough around us to make it clear that we are living in a spiritually foreign land. Human life, that basic gift of God, has been cheapened to the point that people feel free to kill their own unborn children. Human success is measured in bank accounts and notoriety rather than in generosity and self-sacrifice. Human worth has to be proved rather than assumed. Human commitments like marriage are vulnerable to being dissolved when one of the parties decides it's time for a change. We are invited to believe that we are supposed to be comfortable at every moment and that even a headache is somehow unfair. The values and assumptions behind all this, the principles on which our world operates are different from the values and principles of Christ and his Church. Consequently, people who accept the values of Christ are often out of step with the rest of the world. They are different, even as Christ was.

The difference, however, does not lead believers to try to get out of the world or to set up enclaves of safety in which they will not need to be involved in it. In fact, the life of Christ in believers impels them to love the world as he did. It's a good world, deep down, because it's God's world. That's why Jesus came to save it, to give it a new value and a new worth through participation in his life. Our task as believers is to bring the world that life, just as the soul brings life to the body. We may not be high-level decisionmakers or influential guides of public opinion. We may not be important at all, as the world counts importance. But we do have a part to play in the world's salvation, and we play that part by being as consistently, as completely, as practically Christian as our opportunities allow.

Practicing Catholics are people with priorities, the Lord's priorities. They don't necessarily parade their priorities around and make speeches about them, but the priorities are there, and they influence the lives of practicing Catholic believers in lots of different ways. Some of the ways are obvious to anyone who wants to observe them. Some of the ways are more subtle and are clear only to people who choose to look carefully. Some of the ways in which Christian priorities have their effect in the believer's life are known only to the Lord. But the priorities are there, and they are operative.

Of course, they are not the priorities that are shared

by many of the people around us. We may seem to be just like everybody else in many ways, but in the ways that make the most difference to ourselves and to the world around us, we are different. Being a practicing Catholic means understanding and welcoming the difference.

For Discussion and Reflection

- *What do you value most in your life?*

- *Have you ever had to be conspicuously different because you are a Catholic?*

CHAPTER TWELVE

Dying Catholic

Dying Catholic is as much a part of Catholic practice as is living Catholic. It's not that we individually do it often, of course! Yet the way we die, the context of the end of our lives is determined by the whole practice of our lives. At the same time, it is not just our own individual death that is important, but the way we relate to and participate in the deaths of other people. That, too, is part of being a practicing Catholic.

The world in which we live, from which Catholics are different in so many ways, doesn't like to deal with death. It doesn't even like to use the word but finds other ways of referring to it. In our secular culture death has become a biological embarrassment, to be gotten through as quickly, quietly and painlessly as possible, with a minimum of muss, fuss and bother.

Catholics look on death both as the final statement or act of a precious human life on earth and as the passage to a fuller, final life with the risen Christ in heaven. As the first preface for the Mass for Christian death puts it, "The sadness of death gives way to the bright promise of immortality" and "life is changed, not ended."

There are particular external expressions of

membership in the community of faith that are called for at the end of earthly life just as there are for other moments of life. Practicing Catholics want these expressions of faith to be part of their own dying and provide them for their loved ones when they die.

The first of these is the Sacrament of the Anointing of the Sick. The celebration of this sacrament is not limited to the last moments of life, but offers the healing and strengthening action of Christ and the prayers of his Church to all who begin to be in danger of death from sickness, from old age or in the context of a serious operation. It is intended to increase our faith, hope and love at a time when fear and confusion could otherwise turn our attention away from God.

But if the Sacrament of the Anointing of the Sick is given to all those who suffer from serious illness and infirmity, it is particularly appropriate for those who are at the point of departing this life. In that circumstance, it is usually accompanied by the Sacrament of Reconciliation and the reception of Holy Communion as *viaticum*, food for the journey. Practicing Catholics let their relatives and friends know that they wish to receive these "last rites" when their own life is coming to an end, and they take pains to see that these rites are accessible to those for whom they share responsibility. They know that God wants to be with his faithful when they are sick and dying even as he wants to be with them in the rest of their life.

The death of the Christian believer is followed by the funeral. The order of Christian funerals ordinarily has three parts. The first is the vigil, which generally takes place at a funeral home but can also be carried out in the church where the funeral liturgy will take place. This rite is a series of readings and prayers which are intended to help the dead person's family and friends express their sorrow and find strength and consolation in their faith in Christ and his Resurrection. Other members of the Christian community offer support to the mourners by being present and by praying that the one they have lost may have eternal life.

Next is the funeral Mass. At this eucharistic celebration the community of faith offers the sacrifice of Christ together not just the eternal rest of the one who has died, but also as an expression of the link between the death of the believer and the death and resurrection of Jesus. Funeral Masses generally include a homily. The funeral homily is not intended to be a eulogy of the dead person (which is more appropriate as part of the vigil service or the final commendation), but rather an instruction based on sacred Scripture about the Christian significance of life and death and about the meaning of the death and resurrection of Jesus. The participants at the funeral Mass are invited to receive Holy Communion, not only to pray for the deceased in their moments with the Lord, but also to express their faith in the eternal life that we all hope to share with the risen Christ. After a brief commendation ceremony, in which the body is generally incensed as a sign of honor to the dead person's dignity as a member of Christ, the mourners proceed to the cemetery for the rite of committal.

At the cemetery there are further prayers and the body is committed to its grave, the final act of the community of faith caring for the body of its deceased member. At the end, the presiding minister invites the participants to "Go in peace," an invitation that they have heard in many other contexts but which has a special meaning in the context of the peace they have been seeking for their dear one.

In the past, it was not permitted for Catholics to have their body cremated, since cremation was generally used as a sign that the dead person did not believe in eternal life. Now cremation is permitted, but traditional burial is generally preferred as being more in accord with the long practice of the Church and as a clearer sign of Catholics' belief in the final resurrection. Most Catholics want to be buried in a Catholic cemetery as a last sign of their attachment to and gratitude for the community of faith in which they spent their lives.

It's important for Catholics to understand what a funeral is really all about. It is not intended to be an accolade of respectability for a life well lived but an expression of care from Christ and the Church for a member whose earthly journey is now ended. Criminals and saints, popes and paupers, people who went to Mass every day and people who haven't practiced their faith in years can be "buried from the church." All Catholics (as well as catechumens) have the right to a Catholic funeral. You don't have to qualify, as long as you have been somehow in touch with the Church at some point in your life. The point is not that how one has lived or how faithful one has been is of no significance to God and the Church. The point is that judgment is the prerogative of the Lord and that, when the end comes, we must all rely on the kindness and mercy of the Lord.

The way we die and the way we observe the death of others reflects a whole attitude toward life and the value of life. It's part of a Catholic consistency that includes attitudes toward terrible things like abortion and assisted suicide and wonderful things like family, friendship and community in the Lord. Catholics don't believe that you have to cling to life with every conceivable means or that death is the worst thing that could happen to us. They see life as a gift on loan from God that they must care for with good human prudence and use as productively as they can. And when that life comes to an end, they look forward to something even better.

Having a Catholic funeral is a statement, a statement about faith and hope on the part of the dead person, or at least on the part of his or her family, and on the part of the Church. It expresses who we are and what we hope to become. It expresses something about the significance of each and every human life, and in so doing, offers hope for the one who has died and authentic Christian comfort for those who remain behind.

After the Second Vatican Council, the Church's funeral liturgy changed. Before, the liturgy stressed loss and the prospect of judgment. Those elements are not denied in the present liturgy, but they are balanced by a greater sense of God's love and mercy. That's why priests are permitted to wear white vestments now as well as black or purple. A funeral is not an occasion of undiluted grief but an occasion of gratitude, comfort and hope. That's why practicing Catholics want their death to be observed in the context of the community of the Church and why they make provision for the Church's participation in the death of those they love.

For Discussion and Reflection

- *Are you afraid of death? Why? Why not?*
- *What do you think about when you go to a funeral?*

Conclusion

B eing a practicing Catholic has to do with Jesus in our
lives. It is the way we respond to and express two
basic principles that were inherent in the life and
ministry of Jesus and which continue to be operative in
his Church: the incarnational principle and the
sacramental principle.

The incarnational principle is that in Jesus God
became a human being, a true and full human being
with body and soul, with temptations and frustrations,
with emotions and bodily pains. Only sin was missing
in his human existence. Through the incarnation, God
became a participant in human space and in human
time. By means of the human nature that he took on,
Jesus redeemed the world. Since the Incarnation, the
world is God's world in a way that it had not been
before. But the Incarnation is not over. Jesus is still true
God and true man, still active in our world, still offering
us redemption. God still loves us today as he loved us
during the time of Jesus' earthly ministry. The action of
Father and Son continues through the Holy Spirit in the
Church. The Church is not God, but it is the chief
instrument of God's ongoing activity all around us. The
Church works through its members, which means that

those who strive to be active in their faith are both recipients and instruments of God's redeeming action in the world. They benefit from and extend the incarnational activity of Jesus.

The sacramental principle is a counterpart of the incarnational principle. Just as Jesus uses his humanity and ours to bring about his saving activity, so also he uses other created things, things like bread and wine and water and words, to initiate and sustain his life in us. Practicing Catholics understand and appreciate the sacramental nature of Jesus' activity in the seven canonical sacraments of the Church. But the sacramental principle is also operative in the words of the Church's ministers, in the blessings that come to believers through their families and friends, in "ordinary" things like sunsets, rainstorms and the quiet passages of time.

Being a practicing Catholic is not a matter of going through a complicated series of special motions in order to keep God aware of us, but of engaging in a whole style of life that will keep us aware of God, receptive of what God is giving us, attentive to what God entrusts to us to hand on to others. It means being conscious of and responsive to the presence and action of the Lord in the Church, in ourselves and in the world around us. It means taking seriously both the incarnational principle and the sacramental principle. This is what lies behind the practices that I have described in this book.

Not all the practices are equally important. Raising the children Catholic is more important than praying to the saints, and participating in the life of the parish is more important than saying the rosary.

The fundamental Catholic practices are the

sacraments, those extensions of the incarnational activity of Jesus that are expressed in the words and actions that he entrusted to his Church for our salvation. The sacraments are not "things" that we receive but events in which we participate. These events bring the action of Christ to bear on the special occasions of our life, like birth and marriage and death, but they also sanctify our earthly existence day to day and week to week. A believer who is out of touch with the sacraments cannot be a practicing Catholic because he or she has lost contact with those actions of the Lord which imbue our lives with his presence and make them Catholic Christian lives.

There are many other Catholic practices that I have not treated in these reflections, things like novenas and the Way of the Cross and the observance of First Fridays. These practices, and others like them, are matters of personal choice and taste. Every practicing Catholic has his or her own mix of observances which, together with the essential ones, constitute a personalized way of living out the faith. But all authentic Catholic practice is somehow rooted in the principles of incarnation and sacramentality that lie at the heart of our Catholic existence.

Just as there are different styles of Catholic practice, so there are different levels of intensity. Some practicing Catholics content themselves with the minimum, observing only the specific demands of Church law. Others are more fervent. They go to Mass during the week, take on greater penitential practices during Lent, are active and generous in the life of their parish. Obviously a deeper and more developed level of practice is better both for the individual Church member and for the Church community at large. Being content with the minimum is to settle for survival. The Lord invites us to more than that.

Sometimes new devotions or observances arise in the Church, new ways of praying or new emphases on old truths or new manifestations of the action of the Blessed Mother or the saints. Church authorities are generally slow to offer their approval to such things because it takes time to determine whether they are wholesome and authentic or not. Catholics are free to respond to such movements as part of their faith practice as long as these new developments have not been explicitly rejected by the Church, but it is always clear that such new developments cannot substitute for or supersede the basics of Catholic practice, such as doing penance and participating in the sacraments.

Our Catholic faith is a gift. It is an invitation from God to share in the life of his incarnate Son Jesus. And it calls for a response. There is the response of basic acceptance in baptism through which we begin to live the life of Christ and become members of the Church forever. But that's not enough. Our lives change and develop day by day, and our response to God's gift of faith has to be a day-by-day response. That response is constituted by our practice of the faith. Through our habits of prayer and participation in the sacraments, through the way we live our family life, through the conscious way we deal with the blessings and the burdens of our life, through the manner in which we carry out our responsibilities to the Christian community around us, through all this we are responding to God's gift to us of his own life.

Practicing our faith is not just a way of maintaining our identity in a traditional Catholic subculture. It's not a mechanism to earn God's benevolence. It is an ongoing response to God's generosity. And if the response is not made, the generosity will be taken for granted, under-appreciated and soon forgotten.

But that's not all. Our response to God's generosity in the practice of our faith is not just necessary for our individual ongoing spiritual health and vitality. Other people need our response, too. The other members of the community of faith need the example of our response as an encouragement to their own. The simple fact of being with other believers on Sunday strengthens the faith of everybody who is there. The dedication of one Catholic family enriches the life of the Catholic family next door.

But it's not just a matter of example. Since the community of faith is an extension of the one life of the risen Christ, the energy and commitment of each member strengthens the whole Body. The Church needs the faithful practice of its members for the sake of its own corporate well-being and energy.

Finally, the benefit of our practice is not just limited to other believers. We are all called to spread the gospel. You don't have to write books or preach sermons to do that. Simply letting other people see in our practice what our faith means to us is an invitation to them to share it and therefore a blessing for them.

In the last analysis, being a practicing Catholic means living consistently with what we are: ordinary men and women called to share and express the life of the risen Christ as a matter of practice.

For Discussion and Reflection

- *How has the Catholic practice of others been a blessing in your life?*
- *To what extent are you a practicing Catholic?*